I, _____, am committed to becoming an antiracist change maker and doing my part to create a better world.

BECOME AN ANTIRACIST CHANGEMAKER

THE OFFICIAL COMPANION JOURNAL OF ME AND WHITE SUPREMACY YOUNG READERS' EDITION

LEARN HOW YOU CAN FIGHT RACISM AND CHANGE THE WORLD TODAY!

LAYLA F. SAAD

sourcebooks eXplore

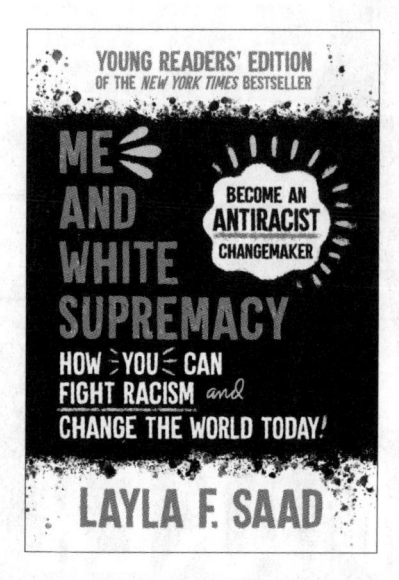

Text copyright © 2023 by Layla Saad
Cover and internal design © 2023 by Sourcebooks
Cover design by Jordan Kost / Sourcebooks
Internal design by Michelle Mayhall / Sourcebooks

Sourcebooks and the colophon are registered trademarks of Sourcebooks.

All rights reserved. No part of this book may be reproduced in any form or by any electronic or mechanical means including information storage and retrieval systems—except in the case of brief quotations embodied in critical articles or reviews—without permission in writing from its publisher, Sourcebooks.

Published by Sourcebooks eXplore, an imprint of Sourcebooks Kids
P.O. Box 4410, Naperville, Illinois 60567-4410
(630) 961-3900
sourcebooks.com

Cataloging-in-Publication Data is on file with the Library of Congress.

Source of Production: Versa Press, East Peoria, Illinois, United States of America
Date of Production: September 2022
Run Number: 5026909

Printed and bound in the United States.
VP 10 9 8 7 6 5 4 3 2 1

CONTENTS

Introduction	**7**
Who Is This Work For?	**10**
How to Use This Journal	**11**
A Little about You	**13**
White Supremacy	**33**
White Privilege	**35**
White Fragility	**45**
Tone Policing	**51**
White Silence	**57**
White Superiority	**67**
White Exceptionalism	**75**
Check-In	**85**
Color Blindness	**93**

Anti-Blackness	**103**
Racist Stereotypes	**111**
Cultural Appropriation	**117**
White Feminism	**125**
Allyship	**135**
Holding Ourselves and Others Accountable	**143**
Your Antiracist Values and Commitments	**151**
Your Antiracist Affirmation	**166**
Closing Letter from the Author	**169**
Notes	**172**
About the Author	**175**

INTRODUCTION

Dear Changemaker,

Welcome to this guided journal, which serves as the official companion to *Me and White Supremacy: Young Readers' Edition*.

As the author of *Me and White Supremacy*, one of my intentions was to make it a book that you not only *read* but also that you *do*. I believe that awareness leads to action, and action leads to change. And that's why I wrote this book. To help you understand what white supremacy is, how it works, and how you can help dismantle it so that we can create a fairer world.

One of the most powerful ways to create awareness is the practice of journaling, which is why it is a key feature of *Me and White Supremacy* and why I have created this guided journal to accompany it.

This guided journal includes all of the reflection questions laid out in *Me and White Supremacy: Young Readers Edition* with lots of space for note-taking and freewriting, and plenty of additional notes pages in the back. It is perfect to use whether you are working by yourself or in a group. And it will serve as an antiracism tool that you can come back to again and again.

As you work through this journal, you will experience a range of challenging emotions like sadness, anger, frustration, and disgust. I want you to know that as difficult as those emotions are, they are normal and an important part of the work of antiracism. In order to change the world, we need to look at white supremacy throughout history and in our lives and the lives of people around us today. And that is really hard to do. But I believe that is the work that we *must* do. And I believe it is the work that we *can* do. However, please know that it is also important for us to focus on more positive emotions like love, hope, and compassion in our antiracism work. We can work together joyfully to create a better world.

    This journal is for your eyes only. And by using it to dig deep and do the work, you are embarking on a journey that many other adults and young people are on too. There are changemakers around the world who have dedicated themselves to fighting racism and creating an antiracist world. You can become one of those changemakers too.

Thank you for helping create a fairer world.

WHO IS THIS WORK FOR?

This book was written for people of *all* races to explore their relationship with white supremacy and learn how they can practice antiracism.

HOW TO USE THIS JOURNAL

GO AT YOUR OWN PACE

We cover a lot of things in this book that may be challenging for you to think about and discuss. Be sure to refer back to *Me and White Supremacy: Young Readers' Edition*. There is additional guidance in the book that will help you work through your responses to the prompts in this journal. There's no need to rush; you can go as slow or as fast as you are comfortable. Remember it's not a competition; it's a journey.

WORK ALONE OR WITH A GROUP

See Chapter 1 in *Me and White Supremacy: Young Readers' Edition* for advice and basic guidelines on doing this work in a group setting.

YOU CAN HELP *CHANGE* THE WORLD.

LET'S BEGIN NOW.

A LITTLE ABOUT YOU

Race: Refers to a grouping of humans based on shared observable, physical features, such as skin color, facial features, and hair textures. Examples of different races include Black, white, Asian, Native American, and others.

What race(s) do you identify as?

Ethnicity: Refers to a grouping of humans based on shared social traits, such as language, ancestry, history, place of origin, or culture. Examples of different ethnicities

DATE:

include Arab, Jewish, English, Dutch, Korean, Chinese, Nigerian, Tanzanian, Mexican, Māori, and others.

What ethnicity or ethnicities do you hold?

Nationality: Refers to your country of citizenship, the country on your passport or where you hold legal rights as a citizen. Examples of different nationalities include British, American, Kenyan, French, Australian, Argentinian, and others.

What is your nationality?

Other than your race, ethnicity, and nationality, who are you? What other important parts of your identity, experiences, personality, likes and dislikes, make up who you are?

DATE:

DATE:

Before learning about race in this chapter, what did you think the word *race* meant?

What do you think the word *racism* means?

What do you think the term *white supremacy* means?

DATE:

What conversations have you had with your friends about race? What about racism?

DATE:

What conversations have you had with your parents and family members about race and racism?

DATE:

What conversations have your teachers had with you and your classmates about race and racism? Have you ever learned about these things in your school lessons? If so, what did you learn?

DATE:

DATE:

Have you ever had any conversations with people in your life about white supremacy?

What things have you heard or seen on TV about race and racism?

DATE:

Have you ever experienced racism? What happened? How did it make you feel?

DATE:

Have any of your friends or family experienced racism? What happened? How do you think it made them feel?

DATE:

DATE:

How does talking about race and racism make you feel? How does talking about your racial identity make you feel?

DATE:

Do you have any fears or nervousness about doing or saying the wrong thing when it comes to racism?

What questions do you wish you could ask an expert about race or racism?

THE MORE WE UNDERSTAND WHAT WHITE SUPREMACY ACTUALLY IS, THE MORE CONFIDENT WE ALL BECOME TO TALK ABOUT IT & FIGHT IT.

WHITE SUPREMACY

White supremacy is a type of racism. It is based on the racist idea that white people are superior to people of all other races and therefore should be dominant over and treated better than people of all other races.

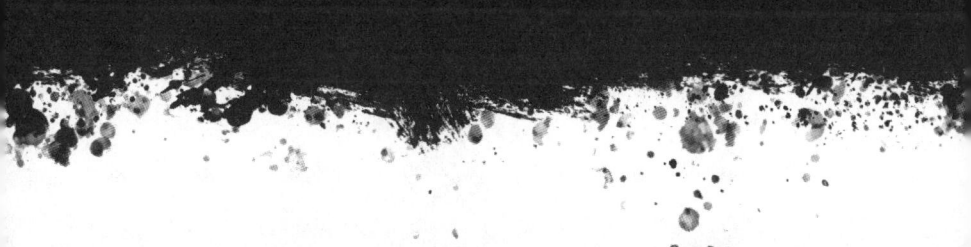

In order to change the world, we need to look at white supremacy throughout history and in our lives and the lives of people around us today. And that is really hard to do. But I believe that it is the work that we must do.

WHITE PRIVILEGE

White privilege is a term that describes the unearned advantages, benefits, and immunities that white and white-passing people receive because of their race.

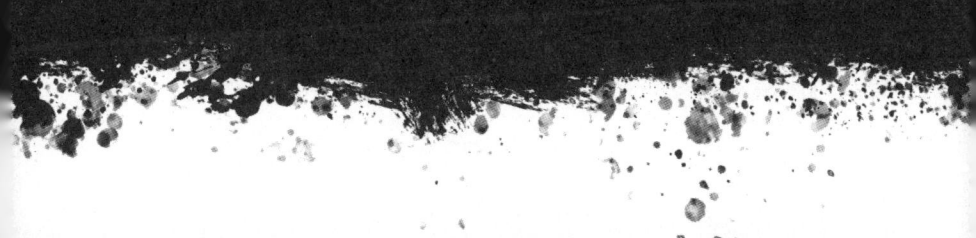

DATE:

Go through the list and note all the examples that apply to you.

- ❑ I have never been told or felt that others didn't want to play with me or be my friend because of the color of my skin.
- ❑ I have never been insulted about my race or the color of my skin.
- ❑ Nobody in my family has ever been insulted or harmed because of their race or the color of their skin.
- ❑ I have never been asked why my skin is the color that it is.
- ❑ I have never been asked where I "really" come from.
- ❑ I have never been told to go back to where I "really" come from. People of my race are never told to go back to where they "really" come from.
- ❑ I can go to stores alone and not worry about being followed or harassed because of the color of my skin.
- ❑ I can play outside or hang around outdoors and not worry about being followed, harassed, harmed, or killed because of the color of my skin.
- ❑ The majority of people on TV shows, in movies, and on the covers of magazines are the same race as me.
- ❑ In school, when we learn about our country's history or about "civilization," I'm taught that it was made by people who are the same race as me.
- ❑ My parents do not have to teach me about my race and racism for my daily physical protection.

DATE:

- ❏ People don't make assumptions that I am less well-behaved because of the color of my skin.
- ❏ People don't make assumptions that I am less intelligent because of the color of my skin.
- ❏ People don't make assumptions that my family has less money because of the color of our skin.
- ❏ I am never asked to speak for all people of my race (questions like "What do people of your race think about this?")
- ❏ I can easily find many different types of toys and games featuring people of my race.
- ❏ If I'm having a bad day, it's never been because of something to do with my race.
- ❏ I've never felt or been rejected or excluded because of my race.
- ❏ I never have to worry if my family members are safe because of their race.
- ❏ If I get a cut, I can easily find bandages that closely match my skin color.
- ❏ The majority of leaders in my country are the same race as me.
- ❏ I've never been told that I can't play a certain character in a school play because of my race. I've never been told that I *have to* play a certain character in a school play because of my race.
- ❏ Nobody ever makes weird comments about my hair, my cultural foods, my cultural clothes, my accent, my parents' accents, or my cultural and religious holidays that make me uncomfortable.

DATE:

- ❏ My cultural or religious holidays are celebrated by the entire country.
- ❏ I've never had to explain my cultural holidays or traditions to my classmates.
- ❏ My school teaches about many people from history who are the same race as me.
- ❏ My parents taught me that we "don't see color."
- ❏ My parents rarely, if ever, have conversations about our race with me.
- ❏ I've never felt or been told that I am less attractive because of my race.
- ❏ Most of the protagonists in the fiction books we read at school are the same race as me.
- ❏ Most of the protagonists in popular TV shows and movies are the same race as me.
- ❏ People of my race have never historically faced discrimination, enslavement, genocide, land theft, segregation, or other forms of oppression based on race.
- ❏ I don't feel very comfortable or confident having conversations about my race and racism, because they are not conversations I have often.
- ❏ I've never been mistaken for another person who is the same race as me.

The more statements that you were able to check off this list, the more likely it is that you hold white privilege.

What positive experiences do you think white privilege gives white people?

DATE:

What negative experiences do you think white privilege protects white people from?

How does talking about white privilege make you feel?

Why do you think society is currently set up to give people who are white or who look white this privilege? Why do you think it denies people who are not white this privilege?

DATE:

Has a parent or adult ever talked to you about what it means to be your race?

WHITE FRAGILITY

White fragility is a term coined by Robin DiAngelo that is defined as "a state in which even a minimum amount of racial stress becomes intolerable, triggering a range of defensive moves." White fragility is the fight, flight, or freeze reaction that many people with white privilege often have when it comes to having conversations about racism.

DATE:

If you have white privilege, have you ever experienced white fragility? If you are a BIPOC, has a person with white privilege ever had a reaction of white fragility toward you?

What did this reaction look like?

How did you feel at the time it was happening, and how do you feel about it now?

How do you think white fragility prevents people with white privilege from really being able to empathize with BIPOC who experience racism?

How might people who have white privilege have deeper friendships with BIPOC if they can change from a mirror reaction of fragility to an elastic band reaction of resilience?

DATE:

WHITE FRAGILITY **NOT ONLY GETS IN THE WAY** OF **ANTIRACISM,** IT ALSO SUSTAINS WHITE SUPREMACY.

TONE POLICING

Tone policing is a tactic used by those who have white privilege to silence those who do not, by focusing on the tone of what is being said rather than the actual content.

Tone policing does not only have to be spoken out loud publicly. People with white privilege often tone police BIPOC in their thoughts or behind closed doors.

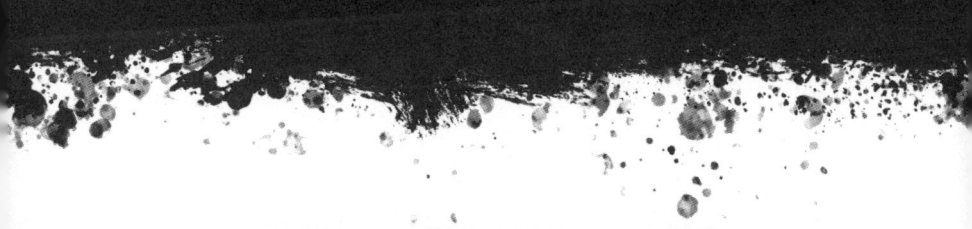

DATE:

If you have white privilege, have you ever tone policed a BIPOC?
If you are a BIPOC, have you ever been tone policed?

Was the tone policing explicit or implicit?

DATE:

How did it make you feel then, and how do you feel about it now?

How is tone policing an example of white supremacy? *(Reminder: white supremacy says white people deserve to be dominant over nonwhite people)*

What emotional and mental damage do you think tone policing does to BIPOC?

WHEN WE UNDERSTAND HOW TONE POLICING WORKS & WHY IT HAPPENS, WE CAN CHANGE OUR BEHAVIORS TO ALLOW BIPOC THE FULL EXPRESSION OF THEIR HUMANITY.

WHITE SILENCE

White silence is when people who have white privilege stay complicit and silent when it comes to issues of race and racism.

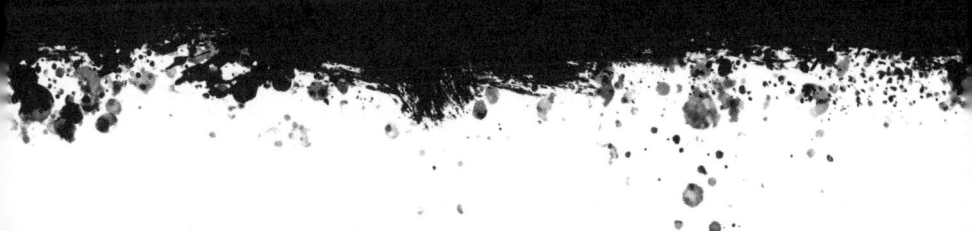

DATE:

If you have white privilege, have you ever been in a situation where you were silent about racism that you were seeing?

If you are a BIPOC, have you ever been in a situation with a person with white privilege who stayed silent when racism was happening to you or another BIPOC?

DATE:

How did you feel about it then, and how do you feel about it now?

Why do you think a lot of people with white privilege use white silence? What do you think they'll lose by speaking up, and what do you think they'll gain?

How does staying silent about racism make people with white privilege complicit in racism?

Who in your life and community may be hurting because of white silence?

DATE:

How do you think the world would be different if more people with white privilege stopped being silent and spoke out about racism?

THE BURDEN OF **SPEAKING OUT AGAINST RACISM** SHOULDN'T ONLY FALL ON THE SHOULDERS OF BIPOC. IN FACT, IT'S THE RESPONSIBILITY OF **ALL PEOPLE** WHO HAVE **WHITE PRIVILEGE** TO SPEAK OUT **AGAINST RACISM.**

WHITE SUPERIORITY

White superiority is the untrue and racist idea that people with white or white-passing skin are superior to and therefore deserve to dominate over people with black or brown skin.

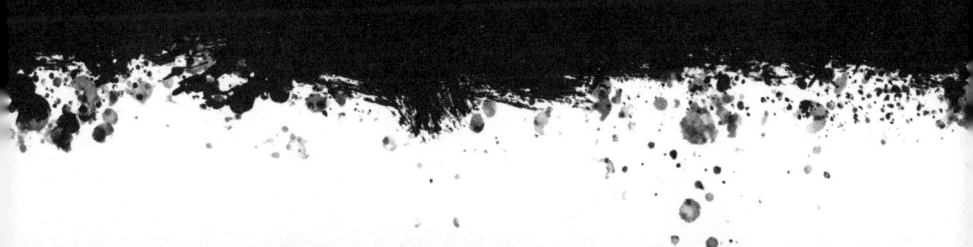

DATE:

What subtle messages do you receive from home, school, TV shows, movies, the internet and social media, or shops and businesses that people with white privilege are superior and BIPOC are inferior?

What do those messages look and sound like?

How do you think messages of racial superiority and inferiority cause harm as people grow up?

DATE:

If the ideas of white superiority and white bias start from a young age, what do you think needs to happen to change that? How can we get rid of this idea? What should children be taught instead?

DATE:

How do you think the world would be different if white superiority no longer existed?

We need to look at white ▬▬▬▬ ▬▬▬▬ superiority so that we can begin to unravel it within ourselves and dismantle it within the spaces around us.

WHITE EXCEPTIONALISM

White exceptionalism is the belief that many people with white privilege often have about themselves that they are not racist, do not have racist thoughts, beliefs, or behaviors, and that they are "one of the good ones." They think that other white people are racist, but they aren't, and that they are excluded from the effects, benefits, and conditioning of white supremacy, so they do not have to do antiracism work.

If you have white privilege, how have you practiced white exceptionalism? If you are a BIPOC, how have people with white privilege in your life practiced white exceptionalism?

DATE:

Read the extract below from Martin Luther King Jr.'s letter and think back on the topics we have covered so far. How has white exceptionalism prevented people with white privilege from truly practicing antiracism? What do you think Martin Luther King Jr. would advise them to do instead?

> *First, I must confess that over the past few years I have been gravely disappointed with the white moderate. I have almost reached the regrettable conclusion that the Negro's great stumbling block in his stride toward freedom is not the White Citizen's Council-er or the Ku Klux Klanner, but the white moderate, who is more devoted to "order" than to justice; who prefers a negative peace which is the absence of tension to a positive peace which is the presence of justice; who constantly says: "I agree with you in the goal you seek, but I cannot agree with your methods of direct action"; who paternalistically believes he can set the timetable for another man's freedom; who lives by a mythical concept of time and who constantly advises the Negro to wait for a "more convenient season." Shallow understanding from people of good will is more frustrating than absolute misunderstanding from people of ill will. Lukewarm acceptance is much more bewildering than outright rejection.*

DATE:

How have the white adults in your life (parents, caregivers, teachers, family members) unknowingly taught or practiced white exceptionalism? For example, have they taught you that as long as you are kind to people of all races, then that is being antiracist?

In what ways have you witnessed people who have white privilege who are nice and kind still say or do things that are unknowingly racist?

What do you now understand is the difference between being nice and being antiracist?

CHECK-IN

We have covered a lot, so this is a great time to stop and reflect on everything that we've learned so far and how you are feeling.

Here are some tips on how to process the feelings that this journey is bringing up for you...

NAME YOUR FEELINGS

It's important to identify exactly what you are feeling so that you can honor those feelings and find ways to move through them. What exactly do you feel? Circle any of the words that best describe how you feel. Feel free to add your own feelings to the list too.

DATE:

Sad

Angry

Scared

Nervous

Annoyed

Surprised

Upset

Bored

Sick

Thoughtful

Confused

Fed up

Hateful

Lonely

Overwhelmed

Curious

Sorry

Embarrassed

Disgusted

Frustrated

Helpless

Guilty

Tired

Ashamed

ASK FOR HELP

Talk to a trusted adult in your life about what you've been learning and how you are feeling. Ask them for help on how to move through these feelings. It would be especially helpful to talk to an adult who has read the adult version of *Me and White Supremacy*, because they'll know exactly how you are feeling.

CRY IT OUT

If you are feeling emotions such as sadness, fear, or even anger, it's very helpful and healthy to cry them out. Whether you prefer to cry alone or with a trusted friend or adult, allow yourself to express your emotions through tears. It is much better to let it out than to bottle it up and keep it in.

WORK IT OUT

One way to express strong emotions like anger is to work it out of your body through exercise or physical activity. Running, swimming, bike riding, yoga, dancing, team sports, or just punching a pillow are helpful ways to express anger without hurting yourself or others.

DATE:

GIVE YOURSELF A TIME-OUT

Do you know why parents sometimes give little kids a time-out? It's so that both the child and the parent can have a moment to calm down, think about their actions and feelings, and make better choices for their well-being. You might not be a little kid anymore, but giving ourselves a time-out can be one of the best things we can do for ourselves. A time-out means putting this journal away for a few days or even more (if that's what you need) and allowing yourself the space to calm down, think about your actions and feelings, and make better antiracist choices for yourself and for others going forward. Meditation or other mindfulness practices are also a great way to give yourself a time-out. There is no rush. Give yourself the time you need.

AFFIRM YOURSELF

Positive affirmations are true statements about ourselves that remind us of our goodness and our worthiness. When reading about white supremacy and doing the reflection questions in this book, you may have started to believe negative things about yourself, for example that you are bad or that you are a victim. These negative beliefs are harmful to us and are not what antiracism is about. Take

DATE:

some time to affirm the good things about yourself. Here are some positive affirmations that can help you. Say them to yourself whenever you notice yourself feeling bad.

I am a good person who is learning how to be better.
I am courageous.
I am safe and secure.
I am important.
I am smart.
I speak to myself with kindness.
It's okay to be angry/sad/scared.
I stand up for myself.
I am loved.
I can do hard things.
I forgive myself for my mistakes.
I learn from my mistakes.
I am strong.
It's okay to be vulnerable.
I can ask for help.
I like myself.
I believe in myself.
I can make a difference.
I matter.
I am a good friend.

DATE:

I am proud of myself.

I love myself.

I am a leader.

I am using my voice to make a difference.

I am a changemaker.

It's safe to express my feelings.

I have an open heart and an open mind.

I learn from my challenges.

I am becoming better every day.

YOU ARE NOT ALONE ON THIS JOURNEY.

THERE ARE **MANY ADULTS** AND **YOUNG PEOPLE** WHO ARE TAKING THIS **JOURNEY** WITH YOU ALL AROUND THE WORLD.

COLOR BLINDNESS

Color blindness is the idea that you do not see someone's color, that you do not notice differences in race, or if you do, that you do not treat people differently or oppress people based on those differences.

DATE:

What messages have you been taught about color blindness by parents and teachers?

How have you noticed people with white privilege reacting when they have to talk about "seeing color" (that is, when they have to talk about race, especially about being white)?

DATE:

Do any of the behaviors we've talked about so far show up, such as white fragility or tone policing? Why do you think that is?

How do you think having a color-blind attitude harms BIPOC?

DATE:

Racialization often classes white people as being raceless, but socially speaking, white people are a race too. What do you think it means to be white? What does society tell us about what it means to be white?

DATE:

Racialization often classes BIPOC as being different, other, or minorities who are not the norm. What do you think it means to be a BIPOC? What does society tell us about what it means to be a BIPOC?

The **BEST** WAY TO **COMBAT RACISM** IS TO **NOTICE RACE.**

THIS MEANS BEING COLOR CONSCIOUS INSTEAD OF COLOR BLIND. WHEN WE ARE COLOR CONSCIOUS WE ARE AWARE OF OUR DIFFERENCES AND HONOR THEM.

ANTI-BLACKNESS

Anti-Blackness is the specific racism that is experienced by Black people and people of African descent around the world. It is defined by Merriam-Webster as being opposed to or hostile toward Black people.

If you are Black, how have you noticed anti-Blackness impacting your Black friends and family?

If you are not Black, how have you noticed anti-Blackness impacting Black people in your community?

If you are Black biracial or mixed-race, how have you seen anti-Blackness impacting you and/or impacting the way you interact with other Black people?

What are some anti-Black stereotypes you have seen in movies and on TV? Are Black people often given specific roles such as the sassy sidekick, the villain, or the magical helper? Why do you think that is?

Why do you think that the majority of protagonist roles don't go to Black actors?

DATE:

How have you noticed Black children are treated by white adults such as neighbors, teachers, and shop employees?

How have you noticed Black adults are treated by business and police officers?

How do you think the world would positively change for all people if the idea of white supremacy and Black inferiority disappeared today?

FIGHTING ANTI-BLACKNESS IS FIGHTING WHITE SUPREMACY.

RACIST STEREOTYPES

Racist stereotypes are negative depictions of wide groups of people who belong to one race or ethnicity. They reinforce the idea that these groups of people are inferior, other, and not civilized in the way white people are, with white people being the standard of what is considered "normal."

What are some racial stereotypes that are popular in your country—implicit and explicit, historic and modern—associated with Indigenous people and non-Black POC?

How do you think POC who are citizens in your country are seen differently from those who are recent immigrants and those who are undocumented? For example, are they more likely to be painted with a racial stereotype if they have an accent from their own country? Why do you think that is?

DATE:

How do you think Indigenous children and non-Black children of color are treated differently from white children because of racist stereotypes?

CULTURAL APPROPRIATION

Cultural appropriation is the act of taking or using something from another culture without the right to do so, because that cultural element does not belong to your culture. It often happens within a context of dominant and nondominant cultures and is used to enhance the person or company belonging to the dominant culture in some way.

DATE:

How have you or do you appropriate from other cultures?

How have you witnessed white people appropriating from nonwhite cultures?

DATE:

Why do you think people appropriate from other cultures, even though they know it may be hurtful?

DATE:

What are some ways that we can show appreciation for other cultures without appropriating?

WHEN WE TAKE PART IN **CULTURAL APPROPRIATION,** WE **IGNORE, MINIMIZE, AND EVEN CONTRIBUTE** TO THE *RACIST HARM* THAT OTHER PEOPLE EXPERIENCE.

WHITE FEMINISM

Feminism is about ensuring that all people of all genders are treated equally.

White feminism is defined by Wikipedia as a term "used to describe feminist theories that focus on the struggles of white women without addressing distinct forms of oppression faced by ethnic minority women and women lacking other privileges."

What was your understanding of the definition of feminism before you read this chapter? How do you understand it now, especially in the context of white feminism?

DATE:

DATE:

If you identify as a feminist, to what extent do you think your definition was about gender only and not inclusive of race, class, disability, sexual orientation, gender identity, and more?

DATE:

How do you think practicing antiracism will help you to better practice feminism?

How does understanding intersectionality help us to better fight for all people?

WHEN WE USE **INTERSECTIONALITY** IN OUR **FEMINISM** WE NO LONGER JUST FIGHT FOR AND WITH WOMEN BROADLY BUT ALSO FOR AND WITH WOMEN AND PEOPLE WHO ARE

BIPOC, POOR, DISABLED, LGBTQIA+, AND MORE.

THIS IS WHAT FEMINISM IS REALLY SUPPOSED TO BE ABOUT— EQUITY FOR ALL PEOPLE.

ALLYSHIP

Allyship is defined by PeerNetBC as "an active, consistent, and challenging practice of unlearning and reevaluating, in which a person of privilege seeks to work in solidarity with a marginalized group. Allyship is not an identity—it is a lifelong process of building relationships based on trust, consistency, and accountability with marginalized individuals and/or groups. Allyship is not self-defined—our work and our efforts must be recognized by the people we seek to ally ourselves with."

DATE:

How have you noticed tokenism being used in movies, TV shows, or books?

If you are a BIPOC, have you ever felt you were being used as a token? If you have a white privilege, have you ever used relational tokenism?

How have you noticed white saviorism used in movies, TV shows, or books?

If you are a BIPOC, have you ever felt like someone with white privilege was trying to "save" you?
If you have white privilege, have you ever felt like you were trying to "save" BIPOC from racism?

DATE:

Why do you think optical allyship is harmful?

Why do you think people, schools, and businesses tend to practice more optical allyship than authentic allyship?

DATE:

Schools are a place of learning, but antiracism is just as much about unlearning as learning. What do you think unlearning means, and why is it important for people with white privilege to "unlearn and reevaluate" their understanding of race and racism?

What are some ways that schools and businesses can build real diversity and inclusion without using tokenism and white saviorism?

THE PRACTICE OF ANTI-RACISM IS A PRACTICE OF ALLYSHIP.

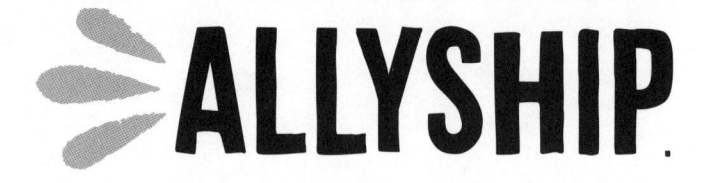

HOLDING OURSELVES AND OTHERS ACCOUNTABLE

Accountability is about being responsible for our actions and the impact of our actions on other people (whether we intended them or not).

What do you think is the difference between canceling people and holding people accountable?

What do you think is the hardest part about holding ourselves and others accountable?

DATE:

How can we make it easier for ourselves to be accountable when we mess up?

DATE:

What are some unintentional harmful behaviors you can take accountability for today?

IT'S GOING TO TAKE WORK TO **CHANGE THE WORLD** AND THAT'S WHY WE NEED EACH ONE OF US **SHOWING UP** AND **HOLDING** OURSELVES AND OTHERS **ACCOUNTABLE.**

YOUR ANTIRACIST VALUES AND COMMITMENTS

Having clear and strong values and commitments helps us show up for the work of allyship with consistency and accountability, which are key for allyship. Our values remind us why we are practicing antiracism, and our commitments remind us how we are practicing antiracism. Each person's whys and hows will be different, and it's important that each of us get clear on what those are for us.

CHOOSING YOUR ANTIRACIST VALUES

Below is a list of common values that can inform our whys. Take a look through the list and circle any that resonate for you. If you have a value that isn't on the list, add it!

DATE:

Leadership

Respect

Making a difference

Freedom

Love

Kindness

Honesty

Authenticity

Courage

Empathy

Resilience

Dedication

Passion

Fairness

Joy

Learning and growing

Being accountable

Caring for others

DATE:

Now, try and narrow it down to your top five values. These will be your top five antiracist values that remind you why you are doing this work:

DATE:

CHOOSING YOUR ANTIRACIST COMMITMENTS

Use the following writing prompts to create your own personal antiracism commitment statement. This is a written statement that you can keep in this journal, on your bedroom wall, on your refrigerator door, in the Notes app on your phone, or in a Google document. In fact, you can keep it anywhere and everywhere you want so that you can easily refer back to it anytime.

To craft this statement, think back on everything we have covered in this journal. Think about what you are ready to commit to in your personal life, family life, friendships, and community life.

DATE:

Use any or all of the following writing prompts to help you craft your commitment statement.

I am committed to showing up for this lifelong antiracism work because...

DATE:

I am committed to challenging white fragility by...

DATE:

I am committed to using my voice for antiracism by...

I am committed to challenging racism in people with white privilege by...

DATE:

I am committed to uplifting and supporting BIPOC by...

DATE:

I am committed to donating my time and/or money to the following BIPOC movements and causes...

DATE:

I am committed to continuing to learn more about antiracism by...

DATE:

I am committed to showing up even when I make mistakes by...

DATE:

I am committed to practicing accountability by...

DATE:

Add any other commitment statements that resonate for you here. And remember, this commitment statement doesn't have to be set in stone. It will change and grow as you change and grow. Come back to it as often as you like to rewrite it as you grow up.

DATE:

YOUR ANTIRACIST AFFIRMATION

You may want to summarize your values and commitments into a single affirmation that helps you remember your values and commitments. See below for some examples:

> I am here to change the world.
>
> I am here to make the world a better place for all people.
>
> I am here to lead with love and justice.
>
> I fight for freedom with courage, kindness, and empathy.

DATE:

What's an affirmation that resonates for you?

NO MATTER WHO YOU ARE

YOU HAVE THE

POWER

TO INFLUENCE

CHANGE

IN THE WORLD.

CLOSING LETTER FROM THE AUTHOR

Dear Changemaker,

You made it!

    After what has been an incredible journey of learning and reflecting, you now have made it to the end of this journal and the end of our time together. But the end of one journey signals the beginning of a new one, this time with *you* as your own guide as you seek to learn and unlearn more and grow as an antiracist change maker.

    You have come a really long way already,

and you should be very proud of yourself. From examining the ways that white supremacy shows up in the world and in your life, to defining your own personal antiracism values and commitments, you have built a strong foundation that will support you as you continue moving forward in your practice of antiracism.

To dismantle white supremacy—this system of oppression and discrimination that has hurt so many people for so many generations—we need all of us. In creating a fairer world, everyone's contribution matters. No matter who you are, you have the power to influence change in the world. Using your reflections in this journal and what you have learned from *Me and White Supremacy: Young Readers' Edition*, start with yourself, your family, your friends, your school, and your community. The rest will follow as a ripple effect of your antiracist actions. You don't have to wait until you are an adult to change the world. You can start right now.

I hope you will. I know you will.

I believe in you, and I thank you.

Your Friend and Guide,

Layla

ABOUT THE AUTHOR

Layla F. Saad is an international bestselling author, speaker, and podcast host on the topics of race, identity, leadership, personal transformation, and social change. Layla is the author of the *New York Times* and *Sunday Times* bestselling antiracism education workbook, *Me and White Supremacy: Combat Racism, Change the World, and Become a Good Ancestor.*

As an East African, Arab, British, Black, Muslim woman

who was born in and grew up in the UK, and currently lives in Qatar, Layla has always sat at a unique intersection of identities from which she is able to draw rich and intriguing perspectives. Layla's work is driven by her powerful desire to "become a good ancestor," to live and work in ways that leave a legacy of healing and liberation for those who will come after she is gone.

Layla's work has been brought into communities, workplaces, educational institutions, and events around the world that are seeking to create personal and collective change.

Find out more about Layla at laylafsaad.com.